Self Est

The Self Help Book for Women and Men eager to improve their Self Confidence and Overcome Self Doubt

Nelly Aaron Smith

Table of Contents

Introduction

We all know that self-esteem, otherwise known as self-confidence, is an essential part of success.

It's high time you stop losing opportunities and start investing in building your self-confidence and overcome self-doubt.

Low self-esteem and self-confidence can leave people psychologically defeated or stressed out. Additionally, it may lead people into making bad decisions, fall into toxic relationships, or inability to make people attain their full potential.

Are you concerned about changing your life and achieving your goals without the obstruction of your internal critics but with a high sense of self-worth and confidence? Then, this is the book for you!

An excessive amount of self-esteem, as exhibited in narcissistic personality disorder, could be off-putting to others, and may also harm personal relationships.

Self-esteem levelled at the extreme high and low ends

of the spectrum, can be dangerous, so ideally, you need to strike an equilibrium somewhere in the centre; An authentic yet positive view of yourself is usually considered the perfect. But precisely, what is self-esteem? Where does it result from, and what impact does it have on our lives?

This book will give you the tools to understanding self-esteem, self-confidence and teach you the techniques to master it effectively; you will learn how to stop the negative and paralysing self-talk and establish daily positive affirmations that will impact your subconscious mind and improve your confidence.

In this book, you will learn the types of self-esteem and their features, the methods of enhancing your self-worth, and many more!

After reading this book, you will simply be a new person with a changed heart and a strong level of inner strength.

CHAPTER 1

What Is Low Self-Esteem

Low self-esteem sometimes appears as inadequate self-confidence, circumstances of feeling terrible about oneself. Individuals who have low self-esteem often feel unlovable, uncomfortable, or incompetent.

Regarding experts Morris Rosenberg and Timothy J. Owens, who published Low Self-Esteem People: A Collective Portrait, individuals who have low self-esteem tend to be hypersensitive. They possess a delicate sense of personality that may be easily wounded by others.

Furthermore, individuals who have low self-esteem are "hyper-vigilant and hyper-alert to signs of rejection, inadequacy, and rebuff," wrote Rosenberg and Owens. Often, individuals lacking self-esteem see rejection and disapproval even though there isn't any. "There's always the chance for them to make mistakes, use poor judgment, do something humiliating, expose (themselves) to ridicule, behave immorally, or contemptibly."

While everyone's self-esteem is vulnerable to other people, who may openly criticize them, ridicule them, or explain their flaws, I'd argue a sustained threat to each person's self-esteem lurks within. Rosenberg and Owens describe, "As observers of our own behaviors, thoughts, and emotions, we not merely register these phenomena in our consciousness but also pass judgment on them. Thus, we may become our most unfortunate critic, berating ourselves mercilessly if we find ourselves passing judgment, forgetting something we ought to remember, expressing ourselves awkwardly, breaking our most sacred promises to ourselves, dropping our self-control, and acting childishly for a moment, acting in regrettable ways that calls for condemnation from people.

This harsh inner critic, whom Dr. Robert Firestone recognizes as the Critical Inner Modulation of voice, contributes to an unhealthy perceived personality. Going about with a weak belief in oneself can have serious effects. For example, if someone feels that other people don't like them, they'll prevent relationships with others and so are quicker to react defensively, cynically, and even lash out. Rosenberg and Owen assert that "the manner with which we hook up with others is usually highly suffering from our self-recognition, regardless of their precision. Indeed, our self-recognition represents probably one of the most crucial foundations on which our social behavior is built."

Furthermore, if we perceive ourselves adversely, whether we label ourselves uncomfortable, unlovable, obnoxious, timid, etc., it becomes a lot more challenging to believe that others can see us in a positive light. "The implication is that to have low self-esteem is to live a life of misery," concluded Rosenberg and Owen.

- Conquering Low Self-Esteem

The glad tiding is that it is possible to overcome low self-esteem! You will see two critical components to combatting this negative self-image. The first is to stop listening to your critical internal voice. While the next is to start practicing self-compassion.

· Stop listening to your Internal Critic

The critical internal voice is usually that inner observer that hurtfully judges our thoughts and activities. This unpleasant inner critic continually nags at us, giving a barrage of mental poison about ourselves and people altogether. It ruins our self-esteem constantly with thoughts like:

- “You’re ridiculous.”
- “You have a fat body.”
- “Nobody likes you.”
- “You need to be quiet. Every time you talk, you only make a fool of yourself.”
- “Why can’t you wind up like other people?”
- “You’re worthless.”

To overcome low self-esteem, you need to challenge this mental poison and endure your internal critic. On

PsychAlive, we have got a whole lot of articles, several Webinars, and an e-course specialized on this subject topic. The first step is to identify when you start having these poisonous thoughts about yourself. Then, you can choose never to concentrate on your inner critic's character assassinations or lousy advice. Maybe it's good to imagine how you'll feel if someone else was saying these things to your face; you'd probably become angry and tell them to shut up or clarify they are wrong about you. Consider using this technique in answering your inner critic.

One way to accomplish this is to write down all of your internal critic's criticisms on one side of the paper. Then write down a far more practical and compassionate appraisal of yourself, alternatively. For example, if you write a self-criticism like "You're ridiculous," you could then write, "I could struggle sometimes, but I am smart and competent."

Challenging your inner critic helps stop the pity spiral that feeds your low self-esteem. When you realize the critical internal voice begin its negative self-attacks, you can defy this inner critic and discover yourself for who you really are.

- Begin to Practice Self-Compassion

Often, the cure for self-criticism is self-compassion. Self-compassion may be the radical practice of treating yourself as being a friend; it is an effective way to create even more confidence in yourself. Research demonstrates self-compassion is way better nonetheless for your mental health than self-esteem.

Dr Kristen Neff, who studies self-compassion, explains that self-compassion isn't based on self-evaluation or judgment; instead, it is reliant on a good attitude of kindness and acceptance towards yourself. While this may sound simple, treating yourself with compassion and sympathy could be challenging initially. However, you will establish more self-compassion as you practice it often.

Listed here are three steps for practicing self-compassion:

1. Acknowledge and see your hurts.

2. Be kind and caring in response to your struggles.

3. Recognize that every human is imperfect.

You will discover more self-compassion exercises on Dr. Kristen Neff's website.

How to Develop Self-Confidence

Research into self-esteem infers that both low and high self-esteem can create emotional and sociable problems for people. While high self-esteem could be associated with Narcissism, lesser degrees of self-esteem could be linked to social anxiety, inadequate confidence, and depression. The healthiest sort of self-confidence is "the moderate self-esteem that's situated more on valuing one's inherent worth like a person and less about comparing oneself to others." With this mindset, in case your goal is to be more self-confident, it is advisable to focus on having a high level of self-worth instead of high self-esteem.

Furthermore, in challenging your internal critic and exercising self-compassion, below are a few other approaches to feel better about yourself.

Stop Comparing Yourself with Other People

Seeking to boost your confidence by comparing yourself with others can be an error. Dr Kristen Neff clarifies, "Our competitive culture tells us we must end up being special and above average to feel good about ourselves, but we can't all be above average at the same time. There's always someone richer, more desirable, or more successful than we are."

If we evaluate ourselves based on external achievements, other people's perceptions and competitions, "our sense of self-worth bounce around just like a ping-pong ball, rising and falling in lock-step with this latest success or failure." Social networking only exacerbates this problem, as people post their picture-perfect occasions and shiny achievements, which we compare to your tarnished, flawed everyday lives.

To have the ability to create a healthy sense of confidence, we must quit comparing ourselves to others. Instead of fretting about how exactly you worth compared to individuals around you, take into account the sort of person you want to be. Map out your goals and undertake activities that are consistent with your values.

Surpass Your Own Moral Code

Self-confidence and self-esteem are rudiments of self-respect. If you live a life that's under your principles and values, whatever they might be, you can respect yourself, be well informed, as well as do better in life. For example, a report at the University of Michigan found that students "who based their self-esteem on internal sources – such as virtuousness or moral standards-were found to have higher grades and less likely to use alcohol and drugs or to develop feeding disorders."

To appreciate your self-worth, it is critical to have integrity and make sure that your actions match your words. For example, if taking healthy meals and looking your best is essential ideals for you personally, you are going to feel better if you continue in such lifestyle. Whenever your actions don't match your words, you are more vulnerable to self-attacks. The inner critic really wants to explain these shortcomings. It is valuable to take into consideration your core principles and act consistently with these beliefs if you're trying to boost your confidence.

Do Something Meaningful

As humans, we tend to feel good about ourselves if we take action significantly by getting involved in activities that are challenging and beneficial to others. That's an attractive way to build self-confidence and develop healthy self-esteem.

Studies show that volunteering comes with an optimistic influence on how people see themselves. Researcher Jennifer Crocker establishes that you get "a target that's bigger compared to yourself." When seeking meaningful actions, it's necessary to consider what's important to you. For some, this may mean volunteering at a homeless shelter, tutoring children, getting involved with local politics, gardening with friends, etc. Follow the clues of where you find meaning, and you will acquire your self-esteem along the way.

CHAPTER 2

Why Is Self-Esteem Important?

Self-esteem reveals someone's values about their worth. Self-confidence is vital because it greatly influences people's opinions and decisions. Self-esteem acts as a motivational function, rendering its help pretty much that individuals can look after themselves and explore their full potential.

Individuals who have high self-esteem are those who are motivated to look after themselves and strive towards the fulfillment of personal goals and aspirations persistently. Individuals who have low self-esteem tend to disrespect themselves; they also tend to let other people's opinions of them get to them, they usually appear timid and diffident in the face of challenges. They could have the same goals as individuals with high self-esteem; however, they're usually less motivated to pursue them with their conclusion about themselves.

Self-esteem is somewhat an abstract idea; it's hard for a person who does not have it to understand what it could be like and buy into it. A great way that people who have low self-esteem can begin to understand what it means to have higher self-esteem is to appreciate the things they value in their lives.

For example, some individuals enjoy cars because vehicles are crucial to them; these people take absolute care of their cars. They make proper decisions about where to park the car, how often to get it serviced, and just how they'll drive it. They could decorate the car and then show it off with satisfaction.

Self-esteem is comparable to that; you take care of yourself, like yourself, and be happy with yourself. When children see themselves as being valuable and essential, they take care of themselves; they make proper decisions about themselves, which improves their value instead of breaking it down.

Sizes Of Self-Esteem

High vs. Low Self-esteem

Self-esteem is undoubtedly occurring around the continuum, and for that reason, it is thought to vary in amount or magnitude from low to high in different individuals. A lot of people have high self-esteem, although some have lower self-esteem. The variations between these people aren't apparent, but instead are evident only through assessment of their thoughts and emotions about their worth.

Proportionality of Self-Esteem: Self-esteem can be thought to vary in another way, which we may describe as proportionality or reasonableness. Since it happens that not all cases of high self-esteem would be the same, a lot of people with high self-esteem have attained that height based on some actual accomplishments. They give themselves credit in maintaining a calm position to meet up with new difficulties because they've had the opportunity to meet up with problems before-hand. Their reasonable opinion of themselves is carried alongside the actual challenges they need to conquer in life.

Alternatively, there are other people whose high self-esteem seems extreme and away out of proportion when evaluated with their actual accomplishments and actions. These people think highly of themselves but cannot show any substantive past achievements, efforts, or opinions they have made, which would justify that high self-esteem to a good-minded observer. Their high self-esteem can be found more on a sense of entitlement than on any achievement. This entitled version of high self-esteem may become less psychologically healthy compared to the greater proportional selection of self-confidence due to the fact that from the selfish and self-centered behavior that may acquire a sense of entitlement. This selection of high self-esteem can also be known as "overly-inflated," meaning that it is extreme and out of proportion to real accomplishments and activities. In adults, this sort of self-esteem could be connected with Narcissism.

Narcissism, like self-esteem, could be an excessive amount of or "overly-inflated" in comparison to someone's achievements and actions; there could also be too low or "under-inflated" self-esteem. Often individuals who have overcome poor self-esteem have mollified adversity and difficulties and treated others well and do have a basis to think reasonable about themselves.

However, for various reasons, including an inclination towards depression, stress, or obsessive perfectionism, a habit of taking part in cognitive distortions, or because they have already been abused or exploited, they could not identify these achievements and activities as significant. They perceive themselves as failing to meet an internalized and unreasonably high standard of goodness and, for that reason, surprisingly exhibit low self-esteem and related emotional stress if they cannot meet that internal standard. However, an observer would see them as deserving predicated on their accomplishments and actions and have difficulty understanding why exactly they feel so terrible about themselves.

Self-esteem is thus more challenging in comparison with just high or low dimensions. It varies both in conditions of magnitude, and in requirements of its reasonableness when put next to achievements and activities. Parents attempting to foster healthy self-esteem within their children have to nurture and cultivate both dimensions. This book will explicitly explain techniques parents can adopt to nurture healthy self-esteem in their children. Before describing these methods, however, you intend to clarify further why wholesome self-esteem, proportional to real success and behaviour and neither over-inflated nor under-inflated, is desired.

CHAPTER 3

Great Things About High Self-Esteem

Everyone wants to end up being happy, successful in life, and achieve their dreams. But what determines our accomplishments?

Numerous mental studies that have been conducted over 50 years back support the fact that success in life pertains to self-confidence. Self-confident people usually flourish in every sphere of life, and alternatively, successful people routinely possess a high amount of confidence.

Furthermore, psychological research reveals that self-confidence is essential for performing any activity as much as possessing the abilities to undertake such task. Confidence is vital to progressing each of our goals, yet many people struggle to build up this quality. They regularly ask themselves if they are wise, attractive, or wealthy enough to be happy, and continue to worry about what other people think of them.

Unfortunately, individuals who have low self-confidence think it is hard to have success. When you have issues with poor self-esteem, you should take measures to overcome it to feel good about yourself and become the master you will ever have.

What's Self-Esteem, and why is it so Important?

Two qualities contribute to self-confidence: self-esteem and self-efficacy. Albert Bandura, a psychologist at Stanford University, defines self-efficacy as people's values within their capabilities to achieve success in a certain way that regulates how exactly they think, perceive, and behave.

Individuals who have a lot of self-confidence consider difficult jobs as challenges to comprehend their skills instead of threats they need to avoid. Confidence enhances a person's inspiration to put more work in attaining his goals and overcome numerous problems and temptations that test his or her willpower.

Self-esteem is our actual emotions and views about ourselves, our self-worth, or personal value. It includes benefits of oneself, and several psychological states - pride, shame, despair, and triumph. It impacts how we believe, act, and connect with other people and how we can live up to our potentials. Self-Esteem determines how happy we are and includes a bearing on our well-being.

High self-esteem creates a foundation for every positive experience in your daily life. It may help you see the positive sides of every situation and appreciate memories. Having high self-esteem is vital in every area of one's life - it pertains to all of the good stuff you could think about:

- better economic standard
- sound mental and physical health
- higher educational achievements
- content personal relationships
- better career prospects

High self-esteem gives you the strength to ask for a will

you've never had, learn from mistakes, and grow.

10 Advantages of Having A High Self-Esteem

1. You are more resilient to troubles and conditions that are inevitable in life. Whenever your self-esteem is high, you discover a way out and skills to jump back from failing, the ability to learn from mistakes and make modifications to improve the problem and overcome the obstacles.

2. You become happy and relaxed with your lifestyle because you respect yourself, and as well have other people's respect.

3. You become motivated in achieving your goals because high self-esteem allows you to trust other people and enhance your confidence and your capability to achieve your goals.

4. You enjoy the company of friends and companions better and attract successful and confident people into your life, who even help to boost your positive energy.

5. You accept new challenges because you are

confident of your strengths and know you can overcome anything.

6. You perform better at any task, personal or linked to your studies or your responsibility.

7. Your lifestyle is even more exciting; you try to maximize every chance, and consider obstacles because you feel assured you can flourish in anything and achieve your goals.

8. You realize that you don't have to be perfect; therefore, you look less stressed. You aren't scared of making bad decisions because you understand that anyone can make mistakes, and it's okay.

9. You'll be yourself and do not have to adapt your behavior, values, and views to meet up with other people's anticipation. You aren't bothered that other people can disagree with your opinions or behaviour. You don't need the approval of other people. You understand that it is impossible to please everyone, so you do everything you consider to be right.

10. You respect yourself and everyone around you. You make a fantastic sociable image that plays a component in your social development.

They are some fantastic things about high self-esteem, but there are tons of more explanations about why high self-esteem is vital for keeping a balanced lifestyle. Confident people have the power to conquer the world; they might be adored by everyone and inspire other folks to look at their examples.

They face challenges of life, take risks, and seize opportunities, they never quit, and they flourish in all they do - at school, socially, in their personal lives, even in their career. When they eventually fail, they see it favorably, they respect themselves, and as a result of this, they are respected by others.

Developing self-confidence: Self-confidence is an excellent skill, and it may be discovered and perfected by anyone just like any other skill. You only have to trust yourself, and other people will have confidence in you and watch your person change for the better. When you have issues with low self-confidence, you should attempt to build up these features in yourself.

You'll find special techniques that you ought to practice each day, and you're sure to become a self-confident person everyone will admire.

Quick Methods to Build Self-Esteem

Gain control of yourself: Don't be too critical by comparing yourself with other people. People are different, and everyone has their value. Make a list of your positive characteristics and their advantages and also build confidence in yourself. Recognize that you are unique and that you truly deserve to be comfortable with your own person.

Take care of yourself and know how to manage panic, stress, frustration, anger, and dread better. When you understand how to handle these emotions, you will also work out how to take charge of your opinions and conduct.

Don't be a complainer: Stop focusing on the complications and problems in your life; instead, concentrate on the solutions and consider making positive changes. Be appreciative of everything – people, the good things in your life, your family, friends, and your achievements.

Identify your realistic targets/vision: Make efforts to achieve your goals and measure the progress you make.

Enjoy positive human relationships and remove toxic people from your life: Spend more time with individuals who fill you up with positive feelings and support you in boosting your self-esteem.

There is no magic solution that can improve your self-esteem and make you a more confident person simultaneously. You need to learn how to feel good about yourself and be comfortable with your person, and this requires a lot of time, patience, and commitment.

Now you understand how to develop healthy self-esteem, so begin to take steps to change your lifestyle, and you will be amazed at the results.

CHAPTER 4

Importance Of High Self-Esteem

The advantages of healthy self-esteem are numerous. Children with high self-esteem come to value themselves and see themselves as worthwhile partners and problem solvers. They strike a healthy balance of liking who they are; while recognizing there are ways they can continue to grow and develop.

With healthy self-esteem, children think they have confident characters and skills; they assist other people, and are worthy of being loved and accepted by others, including family and friends. They experience a fundamental worth of their fair share of resources like food, shelter, love, time, respect, and dignity. Children with healthy self-esteem will be pleased to make and maintain positive friends, and to persevere in difficult situations that occur in relationships, and they'll see challenging conditions as opportunities to try something new; because they like being themselves and consider themselves worthy of being taken care of by others. Also, they are more likely to provide for themselves physically and emotionally and to persist in difficult and effortful pursuits such as, completing their education or mastering an occupation.

In contrast, a low (or reduced) self-esteem is associated with a rise in adverse outcomes. Youngsters with low self-esteem do not usually realize they possess many positive, valuable characteristics and may be ashamed, guilty, sad, or angry with themselves. Because of this, they believe they don't deserve basic things such as food, shelter, love, time, respect, or dignity from others. They could behave negatively; exhibit self-defeating habits, confirming their poor opinion of themselves. For example, they could convince themselves they aren't smart enough to pass a math test. Because they think they can't get good grades, but usually, it is they don't put much energy or effort into preparing adequately for the test. They may also dwell on thoughts about how badly they'll perform, when they fail the test, more as a result of the lack of sustained study effort and anxious preoccupation rather than a genuine inability. This failure is then interpreted incorrectly, but with great psychological "truth" as further proof, they are undoubtedly bad at math. Further efforts at learning math are then discouraged in the wake of failure. This sort of negative feedback of self-defeating thoughts and behaviour may also be known as a self-fulfilling prophecy.

Youngsters with poor self-esteem are less likely to be happy and are more vulnerable to emotional and public problems than their higher self-esteem counterparts. Children with low self-esteem are less likely to persevere through difficult situations because they presume they cannot succeed under challenging circumstances; therefore, they quit too early. They are more likely to be victimized or exploited by others, because they don't believe they deserve to be treated well, or because they believe they lack the skills necessary to escape from their situation.

Children with excessive bloated self-esteem based on a sense of narcissistic entitlement instead of genuine fulfillment may contentedly view themselves as more perfect and more worthy of using special resources than other children, and with that, they become arrogant.

They could be dismissed and, for that reason, refuse to reap the advantages of constructive interpersonal criticism, which other children would leverage on to recognize areas for productive growth or change. They could exhibit "externalization," which means that they could incorrectly assume that others are responsible for the failures they experience; besides they could blame it on not having any skill to improve.

Sometimes children with inflated self-esteem will resort to bullying others because they often think they are superior to others and can treat them just how they like.

Children who struggle with their self-esteem are likely to record fewer achievements than their peers whose self-esteem is balanced and healthy because they hardly want to emerge from their shells, especially when it comes to their ability to create lasting and emotionally satisfying romantic relationships.

CHAPTER 5

The benefits of High Self Confidence

Men and women around the world wound-up with low self-confidence; nonetheless, it doesn't have to remain that way. Studies also show a girl's self-confidence peaks around age nine but wane with adolescence.

In this CHAPTER, we're uncovering several ways high self-confidence can transform your lifestyle, making you become a better person and grow, in comparison to how you have lived previously.

1. Criticism could enhance our growth: Criticism has many facets; sometimes, it's constructive, as every time your manager gently informs you of openings in your field, which may bring about a more definite result when addressed. When considered within this context, criticism is often helpful and healthy.

Generally, criticism seems to be a horrible side-effect of low self-confidence. It could turn spouses against each other, rip families apart, and damage relationships.

Whenever we lack self-confidence in ourselves, it becomes quite challenging to rely on others, and as a result of this, we create unobtainable ideals that even those closest to us can't reach. When you adopt a means of thinking about high self-confidence, you'll readjust your outlook, and give yourself and family room to make mistakes but receive love nonetheless.

2. Stress Becomes More Manageable: According to a recent survey, over 50 percent of working adults have several issues to deal with in their lives that might be causing them stress. From deadlines to family responsibilities and everything you can think of, it could seem funny that we become overwhelmed by things we can efficiently workaround.

Whenever we excuse confidence from our ability to get something done, the weight shifts from merely challenging to all-encompassing and sometimes unbearable, alternatively, high self-confidence helps us muster the energy and determination needed to take care of the most stressful situation head-on.

From headaches and hypertension to libido reduction and depression, stress can play an adverse role in our bodies, by wearing us off at the slightest thought of exhaustion.

Choosing to approach stressful situations with self-assured courage and tenacity can transform the steepest mountain right into a scalable molehill.

3. You can express yourself more clearly: Are there new things in your life you would like to try-out if failing weren't so glaringly an option? Are you itching to convey something but aren't sure how?

The answer doesn't have to be as dramatic as, "I want to attempt skydiving."

Maybe there's a broken companionship you want to mend; but, you are not confident enough to try again. Perhaps you're deliberating on changing your career, but you don't think you have what it takes to go back to college or start all over in the labour market. That boulder obstructing your path is most likely your esteem.

High self-confidence can help you achieve the things you want, acquire what exactly you need, and express yourself with a sense of guarantee.

Studies also prove that a large number of people, especially women in the labour force, are reluctant to negotiate for a promotion. People frequently have a propensity to place the needs of others over theirs. Building high self-confidence can help you shift that attention a little more inward, providing you with the motivation you need to make that crucial first move.

4. Your Relationships become Healthier: With high self-confidence, you won't just treat yourself better, but you're also able to build healthy and strong interactions in your life. If you're sensitive to everything you do and are better prepared to articulate these feelings, you attract the sort of positive energy you produce.

As a result of this, you're also keenly aware of romantic relationships that are more toxic than uplifting, and so you are better equipped to remove yourself from their web if required. From abusive spouses to jealous, spiteful "frenemies," you can spot individuals whose behaviour continues to exacerbate your feelings of self-doubt and loneliness.

There is a primary hyperlink between abuse (in every form) and low self-confidence, though leaving isn't always as cut and dry out as completely cutting off ties.

If you or someone you know is in an abusive relationship, the Countrywide Domestic Violence Hotline offers helpful security intended to liberate the victims.

Listed below are articles targeted at rebuilding finances after escaping from an abusive relationship, providing advice on budget, building credit, and resuming back to work.

5. Setbacks shouldn’t weigh you down: Despite having high self-confidence, you won't be immune to all of life's inevitable ebbs and moves. The simple truth is that despite having all of the self-esteem in the world, you'll likely nonetheless experience setbacks, disappointments, and failures. You may get knocked down briefly, but you'll have the energy to bounce back

up and continue.

With a low self-confidence, the slightest obstacle can feel like a massive blow. When this is the case, each day becomes challenging. Choosing to handle every scenario with self-assurance helps to ensure that whatever hands you're dealt with, you'll bravely confront it. This also provides you with that extra confidence; it heightens your need to jump fearlessly into those big, new, yet, sometimes scary, unknowns.

CHAPTER 6

The Benefits Of Low Self-Esteem

A lot of people tell me I must lower my self-esteem in the act of modesty, credibility, and in a bid to protect the sensibilities of those around me. I wish to heed that advice and be a team player. Still, I'm plagued with lots of rationality that are preventing me from making this become a noticeable difference in my personality.

Before I take any drastic step in life, such as, growing into someone who thinks less of himself for the well-being of others, I must enjoy reaping the numerous benefits and the drawbacks list. I'll concentrate on the advantages of thinking about myself a lot.

It feels great! Regularly! It does increase my testosterone; it boosts my performance generally. Technology agrees that higher testosterone makes muscle development easier. I take more danger. (That's admittedly a combined bag.)

Cockiness places an aphrodisiac influence on some people. (You realize who you are.) Now for the downside of thinking a lot about myself, I discovered even more dangers than I likely should. Higher testosterone raises cancer risks.

Pros of Low Self-Esteem:

Cockiness (until we become malignant anyway), I see my inflated sense of self-worth more as a means of being happy than a flaw. And In the end, I know exactly how to dial-back my self-esteem, but I chose not to.

There is no such thing as the right degree of self-esteem. Everyone who interacts with you will have a different notion of just how much esteem you possess.

Remember that I've succeeded in several fields I had no foreknowledge skill about prior to starting, these include: animations, public speaking, and writing books. These are the experiences I garnered because of my healthy self-esteem.

I've failed in my life and career ten times more than I've succeeded, but my artificial high sense of self-esteem allows me to jump again and keep punching until something good happens.

A few of you will be quick to point the difference between calm inner-confidence and being cocky. But if you think high self-esteem can be masked, you most likely don't know what it is. Once you have a high self-esteem, you lose being clarified. And, if you believe you need to protect your self-esteem, you do not have high self-esteem. That's how self-esteem works.

Benefits of Low Self-Confidence

1. Predictability

By not being confident, you can predict how people will treat you. You know it when people don't acknowledge your presence or don't like being around you.

2. Receiving Attention

When you have low self-confidence, you become unsure of yourself and maybe thought of as been needy. This compels people to want to provide for you, build you up, and making you feel better. You then have the attention you couldn't receive initially.

3. Fitting In

Because you have low self-confidence, you're not likely to be arrogant around people. As a result of this, people will be beneficial to you. Possibly majority of your loved ones or friends are the same way, and this helps you to keep up with them socially.

Drawbacks of Low Self-Esteem

Mental anxiousness or frustration: When you don't like or are not comfortable with the person you're living with (spouse, family, or even friends), anxiousness and depression might set in.

Heavy self-criticism: A chronic condition of self-dissatisfaction leads to an exaggeration of your magnitude of errors and mistakes. And also, you begin to struggle to forgive yourself.

Hypersensitivity to criticism: If you feel attacked constantly, you may close yourself up against constructive criticism. This inevitably means stunted development and progress.

Inability to accept simple compliments: Because you can't deal with criticism doesn't mean you can handle compliments either. You believe people are sincere about the compliments and they are rather out to get you than anything else.

Indecision: The fear of making mistakes leads to inaction on your part, which leaves both responsibility and success to others. Not being able to trust yourself enough because you believe there are no reasons to, and if you don't trust yourself, you won't take steps towards achieving your goals or in fulfilling your dreams.

Perfectionism: This is quite related to indecision, as both are rooted in avoiding to make mistakes, or making a fool of oneself. Perfectionism leads to continuous frustration, and sometimes underachievement when perceived perfection isn't achieved.

Self-neglect: It is the characteristics of humans to love and at the same time overlook whatever we are not comfortable with. Our patterns of self-care, meals, sleep, exercise, cultural interactions - are a reflection of our self-esteem and how much we care about ourselves.

Eating disorders: If you look in the mirror and don't like what you're seeing, inside and outside, at what point do you begin to change what you saw? Sadly, food is used as a pawn in a bid to achieve self-love.

Addictions: When the pain of dealing with oneself becomes too much to handle, habits are adopted to drown out the pain. What pretends to be a "friend" initially quickly becomes a brutal foe. The addict usually doesn't have any self-confidence or willpower to endure it; consequently, the risk simply deepens.

Loss of want: Of most downsides of low self-esteem, none could be more alarming or devastating compared to the increased lack of hope. Low self-esteem feeds you with an over-all negativity about life, and sometimes an inability to relish life or expect anything from it.

Inability to persevere and overcome hurdles when you

have low self-esteem problems aren't just issues; they appear to you like intimidation, and an opportunity to fail.

CHAPTER 7

9 Types of Self-Esteem and their Characteristics

The types of self-esteem can be classified into different levels predicated on the most known and used models: Hornstein's and Ross's - Self-esteem may be the gratitude and respect someone has towards himself which is quite essential to live a quality lifestyle and be successful both individually and professionally.

Self-esteem may be the innate instinct peculiar to individuals from birth, which is changing our lives.

Classification of self-esteem: the nine levels

The first five types are Hornstein's classification while the last three are Ross's.

Hornstein classified the types of self-esteem as steady or unsteady, it lasts through time, whether its high or low.

1. High and steady self-esteem

These types of people possess a firm or high self-esteem since those who have this sort of self-esteem aren't influenced by negative happenings around them. Also, they can defend their perspective in a poise manner, and can keep their head-up for a while without a crash.

2. High and unstable self-esteem

These folks could also be regarded as having high self-esteem; however, they lack expertise in maintaining in for long. They often don’t know how to manage stressful situations, and this tends to destabilize them. They don't accept failure nor do they accept opposing views to theirs.

3. Steady and low self-esteem

These people have emerged as under-estimators, i.e. they can’t accomplish what have set their own minds on to achieve. Also, they may be incredibly cautious and dread making mistakes, and so they'll always seek the support of another person. Nor do they struggle to express their point of view, because they assume they are appreciated inadequately.

4. Unstable and low self-esteem

We're in a position to say that folks who have this self-esteem are those who choose to remain unnoticed, and who believe they cannot achieve anything. They may be very reserved and subjective and may decide never to air their views even when their partner is glaringly wrong.

5. Inflated self-esteem

People with this kind of self-esteem have emerged with robust personalities and assume themselves to be superior to individuals around them. Therefore, they never give consideration or pay any attention to them.

More so, they possess an enormous ego, and tend to blame others in stressful situations. They cannot admit their errors or criticize themselves. They might be seen as being very materialistic and superficial.

Ross Classification

According to Ross, a person might possess collapsed, vulnerable, and robust self-esteem.

1. Collapsed or low self-esteem

Individuals with this self-esteem do not appreciate themselves or their self-worth; this disallows them from feeling too good about themselves. It exposes them to been extremely sensitive to what others might say about them, so if it's negative, it'll harm them, or positive, it'll only increase their self-esteem by a notch.

If a teenager exhibits this sort of self-esteem in high school, he could be a victim of bullying by his classmates.

2. Vulnerable or regular self-esteem

In this kind, the individual has a good self-concept, but his self-confidence becomes shaken especially when met with adverse situations like when someone he/she loves doesn't reciprocate the gesture, or not getting what he/she desires. This will lead him to building defence mechanisms to avoid this sort of position or the need to make decisions since he dreads making mistakes and doing things wrongly.

3. Strong or elevated self-esteem

It includes possessing an explicit self-concept of oneself, strong enough so that any errors committed doesn’t bloat or dent their self-esteem. Individuals who have this self-esteem aren't scared to make mistakes and also have the inclination to possess a high sense of optimism, humility, and pleasure.

How do you know the exact kind of self-esteem you own? Self-esteem is formed while we grow based on our relationship with ourselves and on the environment and individuals around us.

Factors that influence your kind of self-esteem:

- Relatives and friends

Our parents are tasked with building our self-esteem from birth. If they don't have it in mind, they can adversely injure our self-worth by how they address us:

"you are ridiculous" or "you are a disobedient child" etc., are some common examples.

As a child grows, his self-esteem will be strengthened or weakened based on these labels, which is placed by his parents, teachers or friends.

- Strive for goals and objectives

Enjoying healthy self-esteem is something important that has to be present in our life. Obtaining a handful of it gives us the confidence we require and also raise the positive perception, which may positively impact us.

- The attention that's received

Being accepted and popular among people also help us to develop some sort of self-esteem. Then again, being desired by someone you love can be another element that will aid in building your self-esteem.

What's the difference between Self-Confidence and Self-Esteem?

Self-confidence identifies the goal(s) a person proposes and their capacity to accomplish them, while self-esteem is understood as a thorough evaluation a person makes of himself.

How do we improve our self-esteem?

When you have low self-esteem and want to improve it, here are some tips you could adopt.

· Love yourself: Looking after oneself is probably one of the best techniques to improve your self-esteem. Consequently, we must concentrate more on those things that makes us special and unique.

· Don't try to be a perfectionist: Perfectionism doesn't exist anywhere; you will realize there are things people don't know how to do perfectly well, as no one is totally void of errors. Being extremely critical won't benefit us and may impede our self-esteem and our love for ourselves.

· Take failures constructively: Most of us make mistakes, we shouldn't be wary of making mistakes, because if we do not make mistakes, we can ever learn properly. Errors should be regarded as a means to grow rather than personal incidents.

· Collection of realistic goals: We should be capable of achieving our goals altogether, goals that are viable and the short and long-term ones.

Be proud: We ought to be happy with ourselves and what we've achieved because it continues to be the fruits of our work and commitment.

CHAPTER 8

Eight Tips For Conditioning Self-Esteem When Depressed

"Depression often distorts thinking, making a once-confident person feel insecure, negative and self-loathing." Deborah Serani (Ph.D.), a clinical psychologist and author of the publication "Dealing with Depression."

Recent natural thoughts often come as "I am incompetent," "I suck at everything," or "I hate myself,'" according to clinical psychologist Dean Parker, Ph.D. alternatively, "High self-esteem is connected with positive cognitions or values, such as 'I am good,' 'I am successful,' [or] 'I am valuable to others," he said. While low self-esteem could be deeply rooted, you can start chipping away the layers of loathing each time you may take part in an activity that enhances your self-esteem. Below, Serani and Parker discuss their advice on conditioning self-esteem, whether it's low or high.

1. Cope with dysfunctional thoughts: "Research reveals negative thoughts as the linchpin in charge of imparting low self-esteem," Serani said depression also colors your world. "Depression corrodes view and perceptive styles," she said. Mental poison becomes destructive, making you susceptible to poor decisions and abusive situations, she said.

Parker likened this program to an unhealthy mp3 that "repeatedly points out one's failures and self-doubts until one becomes defeated and desire no wish for the future." Coping with these corrosive cognitions is vital. An important strategy is usually to research your opinions for precision. Serani suggested asking these three questions:

"What evidence helps my thinking?

Would others say this is true about me?

Will feeling this way make me feel good or bad about myself?"

This also includes replacing mental poison with

positive ones. But, as Parker emphasized, this doesn't mean repeating empty affirmations; rather, it's about creating and using factual and significant self-statements.

The simple truth is that everyone has strengths and weaknesses. Having good self-esteem means taking and appreciating all your edges. As Psych Central's creator, John Grohol, Psy.D, noted with this piece on self-esteem: "Individuals who have great and healthy self-esteem can feel good about themselves for who they are, appreciate their own worth, and be satisfied with their capabilities and accomplishments. Also, they acknowledge that while they're not perfect and possess faults, those faults don't play a mind-boggling or irrationally significant role within their lives or their self-image (how they observe themselves)."

2. Journal: Keeping mental poison away from your thoughts makes them bigger, Parker said. Writing about these thoughts brings them closer because of their size. Also, it can help you to see the opportunities that exist in your world.

3. Seek positive support: “Surround yourself with individuals who celebrate your advantages, not your weaknesses,” Serani said. Doing this not only make you feel good, nonetheless it additionally “helps solidify positive thoughts,” she said.

4. Create visible cues: Visible cues provide perspective and assist you to curb negative self-talk, Serani said. For instance, she suggests removing negative records around your house and office and keeping inspiring ones on your desktop.

5. Start off your day on a good note: “Discover books, calendars, and websites that are uplifting,” Parker said. Or beginning your day with a dosage of laughter, (Laughter heals) Facebook offers funny memes you can follow. While they could appear simple, these daily acts are another way to produce a supportive environment, he said.

6. Soothe yourself: Both Serani and Parker emphasized the need for nurturing yourself, even though this is the last thing you ever imagine to do.

“Feed your brain, body, and soul with techniques that

make you feel exceptional," Serani said. These ways don't need to be grand (and overpowering). For instance, you might make out time in your day for silence and stillness. (Even several minutes' work, she added.) You might enjoy simple conveniences like "a lovely track or a captivating sunset. Or you might "celebrate everything you currently have instead of what you want", she said.

7. Discover and follow your passions: When you're depressed, your self-esteem feels as if it's sinking day-by-day, it's simple to overlook your passions. Parker advised readers to remember to "write a list of things you enjoy doing along with things you've always wanted to do but haven't done yet."

He gave the exemplary case of a person who believed she wouldn't achieve anything and regularly compared herself to her successful friends. When Parker first asked about her passions, she couldn't identify any. Parker recommended she have a closer look and contemplate her positive characteristics and passions. After writing these down, she realized she wanted to become a fitness expert. Now she's taking programs and working toward her qualification. Identifying and seeking her enthusiasm has boosted her self-confidence and given her a more substantial purpose.

8. Redefine failing, and keep attempting: When you have low self-esteem, it's common to see yourself like a complete and utter failure. But failing is a part of achievement, Parker said. Failing doesn't characterize your being or determine your self-worth.

When Parker coached Little League, he'd show his players that he didn't care if they made mistakes on the field. What he values was that they were swinging and kicking instead of merely standing there.

You will hear countless stories of people persevering despite facing multiple rejections. Consider any author, scientist, designer, or performer. Everyone has encountered rejection at various points in their lives.

As Parker said, "There's no assurance that you will always be provided with positive options. All you need to is one indicator of achievement." For instance, "attending one university out of 10 still allows you to achieve success," he said. "Seize the positive opportunities, focus on the positive responses, and continue," he said.

Conditioning your self-esteem isn't secure. But these useful pointers can help in performing any task. If you were thinking your self-worth is shattered, consult a therapist to build it back up. It's never too late to feel great about yourself.

CHAPTER 9

How to Improve Your Self-Esteem: 12 Powerful Tips

1. Say No to your internal critic

A fantastic way to raise your self-esteem is by learning the best way to handle and displace the voice of your inner critic.

We all have an inner critic. It might spur you to get things done or do certain things to gain approval from the people in your life. But at the same time, it might pull down your self-esteem.

This inner voice whispers or echoes destructive thoughts in you. Thoughts such as:

· You are lazy and sloppy to work.

· You aren't effective in your task, and someone will notice it and throw you out.

· You are worse or uglier than your friends/coworkers/partners.

You don't need to accept this though; you'll find ways to reduce criticisms from the voice and replace it with an upsurge of helpful thoughts. You can transform how you view yourself.

· One way to do this is simply to say STOP whenever the critic arises in the mind.

· You can do that by creating a stop-word or stop-phrase.

As the critic says something – in your mind – you can shout: STOP! Or utilize the best: No, no, no, we aren't going there! Or think of a term or word that halts idea driven by the inner critic.

Then redirect your thoughts to something even more constructive, like planning what you would like to eat for supper or your technique for another soccer game. As time passes, it helps a great deal to find better ways to motivate yourself than hearing your inner critic.

2. Use healthy inspiration habits

To make the inner critic redundant and ultimately boost the self-esteem that helps you to possess healthy inspiration habits, there are many techniques I've used to replace the inner critic in my mind, they may be:

Remind yourself of the huge benefits: An easy but powerful way to motivate yourself and to maintain that inspiration daily is usually by writing down the benefits you get e.g. a new route, or reaching a target.

· Whenever your goal is achieved, note it down and then save the note and put it someplace where you can see it every day, for example, on your workspace or on your fridge.

· Refocus on doing things you enjoy. When you truly enjoy doing something, your motivation for doing that thing would come naturally. When you wish for something in life, you drive through any internal resistance you might encounter to get it done.

· If you drop your inspiration, ask: Am I working towards my goals and self-fulfillment? If not, refocus and begin to concentrate on those things that are important to you.

· Once you've adopted your stop-word or phrase, focus on the techniques. After a while, it will become a habit and your internal critic will pop-up less often.

3. Take a two minute self-appreciation break

This habit is fairly simple and fun, and if you can spend just two minutes doing it each day for a month, it would make a significant difference.

Here’s what to do:

· Take a breath, decelerate, and also ask yourself this question: what are the three things I possibly could appreciate about myself?

Several examples that have proven to be useful when tried out are:

- Support several people each day.

- Help to make people laugh and forget their troubles.

- I am very thoughtful and caring when it comes to our pet (cats).

These things don't have to be significant; you might have listened to someone who needed it today. Taking a healthy walk or bicycle trip after work, instead of lazing around.

These brief breaks usually do not just build self-esteem as time passes but may also turn an unhealthy mood around and fill you with lots of positive energy.

4. Write down three things you value about yourself

This is a variation of the habit above, combining all these could be powerful for boosting your self-esteem every day, or you may opt for this variance by the end of your day when you have some free time to spare.

All you have to do is to ponder on the question from your last session:

What are the three things I appreciate about myself? Write down your answers every night in a journal or on your computer/smart phone.

A tremendous benefit of writing it down is that after a week or two, you can go through all the answers to stay positive and continue to build your self-esteem.

5. Do the right thing

When you do what is right, you not only raise your self-esteem but you also strengthen it.

Maybe it's just a little thing like going to the gym, become understanding instead of being judgmental, or to stop being worried or sorry for yourself and focusing on the opportunities around you and being grateful for everything you have.

It isn't always easy to achieve, or to decipher what the right thing is. One tip which makes it easier to do the right thing is to try and have several of such activities daily. Such as giving someone a chance at having a healthy meal, train somebody or even listen to them.

6. Displace perfectionism

Few habits are often as harmful in life as perfectionism. It might hinder you from taking action because you dread not living up to standard, so you procrastinate, and do not acquire the results you need. This can drain your self-esteem, or you embark on an activity and you become very uncomfortable with your performance and even the results. Subsequently, your opinions and thoughts about yourself are increased negatively plus your motivation to get things done plummets.

How do you overcome perfectionism?

Few things that helped me are:

· Go for sufficiency: When you aim for superiority, you usually have to deal with an incomplete task or activity. Understand that there is something called sufficiency; your task becomes completed when you get to that state.

· Understand that buying into myths about excellence will harm you and the people in your life: This simply reminds us that life is nothing like what we see in a movie, a track, or a book. All these could be sources to consider when you daydream about quality or some superficial things. Reality can crash your expectations if they are picked from any of the sources above. These lofty expectations can ruin relationships, careers, business partnership etc.

7. Handle mistakes and errors positively: If you step out of your comfort zone, or you try to accomplish something meaningful, you are bound to make mistakes and stumble along the way. Failing is definitely okay, it is normal. It is what all those who took action throughout different ages encountered.

So, when you stumble try this:

· Be your own best friend - Rather than berating yourself, think: How would my friend, mother or father support me and help me understand the lesson in this? Then do those things they would have advised you to do and talk to yourself as they would. It prevents you from dropping right into a pit of despair and helps you to become even more constructive

· Discover the upside - Another way to become even more constructive in this kind of situation is to be optimistic and focus on the opportunities.

So think: just what will I gain out of this? And what's one lesson I can imbibe from this challenge? This can change your perspective and allows you to see things differently.

8. Be kind to other people

If you're compassionate about others, you tend to treat yourself kindly and with respect too. And how you treat people is the exact way they will treat you on the long run. So be intentional about being kind to people on a daily basis.

For instance:

- Listen to someone talk about their problems.
- Hold the door for someone.
- Allow someone into your lane while driving.
- Encourage a pal, an associate or a relative when they are feeling depressed or uncertain about life.
- Devote time to helping someone out in a practical way.

9. Try something new

When you try something new or you solve a problem in a little or even significant way and step out of your comfort zone, your self-worth increases. You probably didn't do what you did in a unique or perfect way, but you at least tried something out rather than cuddling your hands in your laps and waiting for things to happen.

So, step out of your comfort zone more often. Don't expect things to happen while you aren't taking steps, constantly remind yourself to try something new, and when you eventually carry out such task, you'll realize that not only does your self-confidence increases but your ability to make things happen also surges.

10. Resist the urge to compare yourself with others.

When you compare your life and everything in it with other people's lives and what they have, you begin to develop a destructive habit. More often, there is always someone who has more of what you have, and someone whose ability surpasses yours in the world.

So, always resist the urge to make comparisons; rather take a look at the heights you've attained and compare your past with your present. Ponder on all you've been able to accomplish, your achievements, results and how you can better work on yourself.

In fact, if there's anyone to compare yourself with, it should be YOU!

11. Spend more time with supportive people (and less time with damaging people)

While you focus on being kind to other people (and yourself) and putting off a habit of perfectionism, it will be difficult to keep up your self-esteem if the people you interact with daily constantly tear down your self-esteem. If your circle of influence comprises of people who are perfectionists, it's high time you let them out of your circle. Reshuffle your circle and ensure that you have lesser interactions with perfectionists or those who are unkind and unsupportive of your dreams and goals. Meanwhile, spend quality time with people who uplift your spirit and those who are generally concerned about you.

Spend less time on the internet; and reading books or watching TV-shows that makes you uncertain of yourself and that can depreciate your self-worth.

Devote quality time to reading books, visiting blogs and websites, and listening to podcasts that can add value to you and increase your self-confidence.

12. Remember the importance of high self-esteem

Remind yourself of the importance of having a high-esteem has stated earlier in this book, in order to remain unshaken and constantly motivated as well as maintaining a balanced self-esteem.

Realizing this and keeping these compelling reasons in mind did amazing things for me. I hope it does for you too.

CHAPTER 10

Ten Ways Of Enhancing Your Self-Esteem

1. Be nice to yourself

That little voice that tells you're killing it (or not), might be a lot stronger than it may seem. Endeavour to be nice to yourself and if you experience slip ups, try to resolve any mental poison. An excellent guideline is to talk to yourself just like you'd do to your friends. That might be hard initially, but practice makes perfect. If you want additional tips, take a look at our approaches on speaking to yourself.

2. Be yourself

Comparing yourself to people is one of the easiest ways to having an inferiority complex. Try to focus on your goals and accomplishments, rather than evaluating yourself with someone else. Nobody needs that kind of pressure to grow!

3. Get moving

Exercise is an excellent way to improve inspiration, to practice environmental goals, and build self-confidence. Breaking perspiration also enables the body to release endorphin – the hormone that makes you feel good.

4. Nobody's perfect

Always try to be the best version of yourself, but it's also vital that you understand that perfection is an unrealistic goal.

5. Understand that mistakes are part of our lives

You've got to make mistakes in order to learn and grow, so do not berate yourself when it happens, for example, if you forget to press CTRL+S on a super-important task. Relax! Don't beat yourself up over it. Everyone's been there.

6. Concentrate on things within your radar

Concentrate your energy on things you enjoy and perform effortlessly.

7. Do what makes you happy

If you spend time doing what you like, you're more likely to build up positively. Create time for this special activity you enjoy on your schedule, it might be reading, cooking, lying on the couch for a while, etc. if it gives you some sort of peace and tranquility, make time for it.

8. Celebrate the little wins

You arrived early today! You poached your eggs perfectly well! Celebrating small victories is an excellent way to birth confidence and have a great sense of self-worth.

9. Be a friend

Being helpful and considerate to other people will undoubtedly make them feel better, but it'll also make you feel excellent about yourself

10. Encompass yourself with a supportive squad

Find individuals who make you feel good about yourself and avoid those who tend to rip you off your self-worth.

Acknowledgements

The Glory of this book success goes to God Almighty and my beautiful Family, Fans, Readers & well-wishers, Customers, and Friends for their endless support and encouragement.

CPSIA information can be obtained
at www.ICGtesting.com
Printed in the USA
BVHW041121160221
600245BV00011B/381

9 781637 501177